Easy Rutabagas Cookbook

50 Delicious Rutabagas Recipes

By
BookSumo Press

Published by
http://www.booksumo.com

LEGAL NOTES

Table of Contents

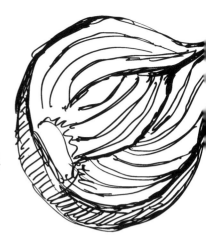

Pot Roast Skillet 54

Parisian Veggie Bake 55

Cold Winter Chowder 57

Carrots, Harissa, Peppers, Chicken, and Sausage Couscous 58

Rutabaga Stew 59

Honey Rutabaga Couscous 60

Homemade Harissa 61

Homemade Harissa 62

Parmesan Rutabaga

Prep Time: 10 mins
Total Time: 50 mins

Servings per Recipe: 4
Calories	372 kcal
Fat	34.7 g
Carbohydrates	10.1g
Protein	6.9 g
Cholesterol	163 mg
Sodium	372 mg

Ingredients

1 rutabaga, peeled and cubed
3 tbsp butter
1 C. heavy whipping cream
1/2 C. grated Parmesan cheese
1/4 tsp ground nutmeg

salt to taste
1 egg yolk

Directions

1. In a large pan of boiling water, cook the rutabaga for about 30 minutes.
2. Drain well and keep aside.
3. In a pan, melt the butter on medium heat.
4. Add the heavy cream and bring to a simmer, stirring continuously.
5. Stir in the Parmesan cheese, nutmeg, and salt and simmer for about 3 minutes, stirring continuously.
6. Add the egg yolk and simmer for about 3 minutes, beating continuously.
7. Add the rutabaga and stir till coated with sauce completely.

SWEET ASIAN
Rutabagas

Prep Time: 5 mins
Total Time: 55 mins

Servings per Recipe: 3

Calories	348 kcal
Fat	15.9 g
Carbohydrates	50g
Protein	5.3 g
Cholesterol	41 mg
Sodium	348 kcal

Ingredients

1/4 C. butter
6 tbsp brown sugar
1 C. hot water

6 tbsp soy sauce
1 large rutabaga, peeled and cubed

Directions

1. In a large skillet, melt the butter on low heat and cook the brown sugar till it is dissolved, stirring continuously.
2. Stir in the water and soy sauce and increase the heat to medium-high.
3. Bring to a boil.
4. Stir in the chopped rutabaga and again bring to a boil.
5. Reduce heat to low and simmer, uncovered for about 45 minutes, stirring occasionally.

Mumtaz Stew

🥣 Prep Time: 20 mins
🕐 Total Time: 4 hrs 25 mins

Servings per Recipe: 15
Calories	111 kcal
Fat	2.1 g
Carbohydrates	12.9 g
Protein	10.7 g
Cholesterol	23 mg
Sodium	80 mg

Ingredients

1 tbsp vegetable oil
1 1/2 lb. chicken, diced
4 rutabagas, peeled and diced
4 medium beets, peeled and diced
4 carrots, diced

3 stalks celery, diced
1 red onion, diced
water, to cover

Directions

1. In a Dutch oven, heat the oil on medium heat and sear the chicken for about 3-5 minutes.
2. Add the rutabagas, beets, carrots, celery, red onion and enough water to cover the chicken mixture.
3. Reduce the heat to low and simmer for at least 4 hours, adding more water if required.

RUTA-ROAST

Prep Time: 10 mins
Total Time: 50 mins

Servings per Recipe: 10	
Calories	299 kcal
Fat	19.2 g
Carbohydrates	20.9 g
Protein	11.5 g
Cholesterol	56 mg
Sodium	407 mg

Ingredients

6 C. cubed rutabaga
1/2 C. butter
1 tbsp minced garlic
1/2 C. all-purpose flour
4 C. milk
2 C. shredded Cheddar cheese
1/4 tsp cayenne pepper

salt and ground black pepper to taste
1/2 C. seasoned bread crumbs
1 pinch paprika for garnish

Directions

1. In a large pan of salted water, add the rutabaga on high heat and bring to a boil.
2. Reduce the heat to medium-low and simmer for about 10-15 minutes.
3. Drain well.
4. Set your oven to 425 degrees F and grease a 13x9-inch baking dish.
5. In a pan, melt the butter on medium heat and sauté the garlic for about 5 minutes.
6. Add the flour and beat till smooth.
7. Slowly, add the milk, continuously and cook for about 5 minutes.
8. Stir in the Cheddar cheese and cook for about 3 minutes, stirring continuously.
9. Stir in the cayenne pepper, salt, and black pepper and remove from the heat.
10. Arrange the cooked rutabaga into the prepared baking dish and top with the cheese sauce evenly.
11. Spread the bread crumbs and paprika on top evenly.
12. Cook in the oven for about 20-25 minutes.

Thursday's
Salad

Prep Time: 15 mins
Total Time: 35 mins

Servings per Recipe: 6
Calories	330 kcal
Fat	12.3 g
Carbohydrates	44.2g
Protein	11.7 g
Cholesterol	0 mg
Sodium	89 mg

Ingredients

1 rutabaga, peeled and cut into 1/4-inch chunks
2 C. water
1 tbsp vegetable oil
1 1/2 C. couscous
1/2 C. nutritional yeast
1/4 C. vegetable oil
1/4 C. apple cider vinegar
1 1/2 tsp honey

1 tsp Italian seasoning
1 tsp dried oregano
1 tsp dried dill weed
1/2 tsp ground black pepper
1/4 tsp cayenne pepper
1 pinch salt to taste (optional)

Directions

1. Arrange a steamer basket in a pan and add enough water to just below the bottom of the steamer then bring to a boil.
2. Add the rutabaga and steam for about 10 minutes.
3. In another pan, add 2 C. of the water and 1 tbsp of the vegetable oil and bring to a boil.
4. Remove from the heat and immediately, stir in the couscous.
5. Cover the pan tightly and keep aside for about 14 minutes.
6. Uncover and with a fork, fluff it.
7. In a large bowl, add the nutritional yeast, 1/4 C. of the vegetable oil, apple cider vinegar, honey, Italian seasoning, oregano, dill, salt, black pepper and cayenne pepper and beat till well combined.
8. Add the rutabaga and couscous and gently, stir to combine.

MONTANA
Casserole

Prep Time: 10 mins
Total Time: 1 hr

Servings per Recipe: 10
Calories	97 kcal
Fat	2.7 g
Carbohydrates	17.5g
Protein	2.2 g
Cholesterol	6 mg
Sodium	65 mg

Ingredients

4 rutabagas
4 carrots
2 tbsp white sugar

2 tbsp butter
1/8 C. milk

Directions

1. Peel the rutabagas and then cut into large sized cubes.
2. In a large pan of salted boiling water, cook the rutabaga till fork tender.
3. Drain well.
4. In a large bowl, add the rutabagas, grated carrots, sugar and butter and mash till well combined.
5. Transfer the mixture into a baking dish and place, covered in oven at low temperature to keep warm.

Lunch Box
Fries

🥣 Prep Time: 10 mins
🕐 Total Time: 40 mins

Servings per Recipe: 4

Calories	50 kcal
Fat	1.4 g
Carbohydrates	8.7g
Protein	1.3 g
Cholesterol	0 mg
Sodium	20 mg

Ingredients

1 rutabaga, peeled and cut into spears
1 tsp olive oil
4 sprigs fresh rosemary, minced

3 cloves garlic, minced
1 pinch salt to taste

Directions

1. Set your oven to 400 degrees F before doing anything else.
2. In a large bowl, add the rutabaga spears, oil, minced rosemary, garlic and salt and toss to coat well.
3. Place the rutabaga spears onto a baking sheet in a single layer.
4. Cook in the oven for about 30 minutes.

HOLIDAY
Puree

Prep Time: 20 mins
Total Time: 10 hrs 5 mins

Servings per Recipe: 6

Calories	220 kcal
Fat	16.3 g
Carbohydrates	16.9g
Protein	4.6 g
Cholesterol	83 mg
Sodium	784 mg

Ingredients

4 carrots, peeled and cut into 1/2-inch chunks
1 rutabaga, peeled and cut into 1/2-inch chunks
1/2 onion, chopped
1 1/2 C. chicken stock
1/4 C. butter, divided
1 tbsp brown sugar

1 pinch freshly grated nutmeg
2 eggs, slightly beaten
1 tbsp all-purpose flour
2 tbsp baking powder
salt and ground black pepper to taste
1/2 C. finely chopped pecans

Directions

1. In a large pan, mix together the carrots, rutabaga, onion, chicken stock, 3 tbsp of the butter, brown sugar and nutmeg and bring to a boil.
2. Reduce the heat and simmer, partially covered for about 45 minutes, stirring occasionally.
3. With a slotted spoon, transfer vegetables into a food processor.
4. Cook the remaining broth mixture on high heat for about 2-3 minutes, stirring continuously.
5. Add the broth mixture in the food processor with vegetables and pulse till very smooth.
6. Transfer the vegetable mixture into a bowl and keep aside in the room temperature to cool.
7. In the bowl, of pureed vegetable mixture, add the eggs, flour, baking powder, salt and pepper and mix well.
8. Transfer the mixture into a casserole dish.
9. In a small pan, melt the remaining 1 tbsp of butter on low heat and toast the pecans for about 1-2 minutes.
10. Arrange the buttered pecans around the edges of the vegetable mixture, creating a border.
11. With a plastic wrap, cover the casserole dish and refrigerate for at least 8 hours.

12. Remove the casserole dish from the refrigerator and keep in room temperature for about 30 minutes before baking.

13. Set your oven to 350 degrees F.

14. Remove the plastic wrap from the casserole dish and cook in the oven for about 30 minutes.

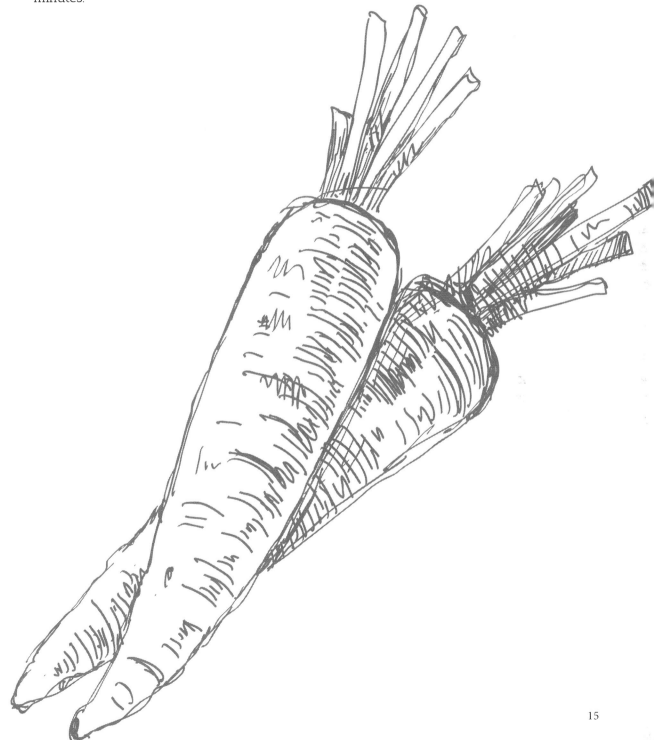

4-INGREDIENT
Mash

Prep Time: 15 mins
Total Time: 40 mins

Servings per Recipe: 6
Calories	144 kcal
Fat	10.4 g
Carbohydrates	10.6g
Protein	3.2 g
Cholesterol	20 mg
Sodium	170 mg

Ingredients

3 slices turkey bacon, chopped
2 rutabagas, peeled and diced
2 tbsp butter

salt and ground black pepper to taste

Directions

1. Heat a skillet on medium heat and cook the bacon for about 10 minutes.
2. Transfer the bacon onto a paper towel lined plate to drain.
3. Drain the excess grease from the skillet, reserving just 1-2 tbsp.
4. In a large pan of boiling water, cook the rutabaga for about 15-20 minutes.
5. Drain well and return to the pan.
6. Add the reserved bacon grease, butter, salt, and pepper into rutabagas and with an electric mixer, blend till smooth.
7. Stir in the cooked bacon and serve.

Cassandra's
Casserole

🥣 Prep Time: 20 mins

🕐 Total Time: 1 hr

Servings per Recipe: 9	
Calories	361 kcal
Fat	16.2 g
Carbohydrates	49 g
Protein	8 g
Cholesterol	44 mg
Sodium	229 mg

Ingredients

7 C. low-chicken broth
3 lb. potatoes, peeled and cubed
1 1/2 lb. rutabagas, peeled and cubed
1 1/4 lb. parsnips, peeled and cut into 1
1/2 inch pieces
8 cloves garlic
1 bay leaf
1 tsp dried thyme
3/4 C. butter, softened

3 onions, thinly sliced
salt to taste
ground black pepper to taste

Directions

1. In a large pan, mix together the chicken broth, potatoes, rutabagas, parsnips, cloves, bay leaf and thyme and bring to a boil.
2. Reduce the heat and simmer, partially covered for about 30 minutes.
3. Drain well.
4. Transfer vegetable mixture into a large bowl with 1/2 C. of the butter, salt and pepper and with an electric mixer, beat till mashed but still chunky.
5. Transfer mashed vegetable mixture into a buttered 13x9x2-inch baking dish.
6. Set your oven to 375 degrees F.
7. In a heavy large skillet, melt the remaining 1/4 C. of butter on medium-high heat and sauté the onions for about 5 minutes.
8. Reduce the heat to medium-low and cook for about 15 minutes.
9. Stir in the salt and pepper and remove from the heat.
10. Place the onions over the mashed vegetables evenly.
11. Cook in the oven for about 25 minutes.

NAPOLEONIC
Soup

Prep Time: 20 mins
Total Time: 1 hr

Servings per Recipe: 6
Calories	236 kcal
Fat	5.6 g
Carbohydrates	36.9g
Protein	11.2 g
Cholesterol	0 mg
Sodium	438 mg

Ingredients

2 tbsp olive oil
1 large onion, diced
2 carrots, peeled and sliced
2 parsnips, peeled and sliced
1 golden beet, peeled and diced
1/2 large rutabaga, diced
1 bulb. fennel, diced
4 C. vegetable broth

1 C. dried lentils
1/4 tsp dried thyme
2 bay leaves
1 bunch fresh parsley, finely chopped
salt and ground black pepper to taste

Directions

1. In a large pan, heat the olive oil on medium heat and cook the onion, carrots, parsnips, beet, rutabaga, and fennel for about 5 minutes.
2. Stir in the vegetable broth and bring to a boil.
3. Stir in the lentils, dried thyme, bay leaves and parsley.
4. Reduce the heat to low and simmer for about 35 minutes.
5. Stir in the salt and ground black pepper and serve.

Buddha's
Delight

Prep Time: 35 mins
Total Time: 1 hr 25 mins

Servings per Recipe: 8
Calories	273 kcal
Fat	2.9 g
Carbohydrates	58.7g
Protein	7.6 g
Cholesterol	0 mg
Sodium	275 mg

Ingredients

3 medium red potatoes, cut into 1-inch pieces
2 C. peeled baby carrots
1 lb. celery root (celeriac), peeled and cut into 1-inch pieces
2 (3 lb.) rutabaga, peeled and cut into 1-inch pieces
2 medium red onions, peeled and cut into 8 wedges each

2 medium parsnips, peeled and cut into 1-inch pieces
5 cloves garlic, cut into thin slices
1 tbsp chopped fresh rosemary leaves or fresh thyme leaves
1 tbsp olive oil
1 C. Swanson(R) Vegetable Broth

Directions

1. Set your oven to 425 degrees F and grease a roasting pan with the vegetable cooking spray.
2. In the prepared roasting pan, mix together the potatoes, carrots, celery root, rutabaga, onions, parsnips, garlic, rosemary and oil.
3. Cook in the oven for about 30 minutes.
4. Place the broth over the vegetables and stir well.
5. Cook in the oven for about 20 minutes.
6. Serve with a sprinkling of the salt.

CABBAGE
and Orzo Dinner

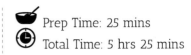

Prep Time: 25 mins
Total Time: 5 hrs 25 mins

Servings per Recipe: 6
Calories   236 kcal
Fat   1.1 g
Carbohydrates   48.9 g
Protein   9 g
Cholesterol   < 1 mg
Sodium   182 mg

Ingredients

1/4 large head cabbage, chopped
1/4 large rutabaga, diced
1 1/2 C. uncooked orzo pasta
1/2 large onion, finely chopped
1 whole head garlic, peeled and minced

3 tbsp chopped fresh dill
6 C. water
2 C. vegetable broth

Directions

1. In a slow cooker, add all the ingredients.
2. Set the slow cooker on Low and cook, covered for about 5-9 hours.

Trinity Soup

 Prep Time: 40 mins
Total Time: 4 hrs 20 mins

Servings per Recipe: 6
Calories	276 kcal
Fat	7.2 g
Carbohydrates	47.1g
Protein	8 g
Cholesterol	5 mg
Sodium	92 mg

Ingredients

1 roast turkey carcass, cut into pieces
12 C. cold water
3 stalks celery, chopped
2 carrots, chopped
1 Spanish onion, chopped
1/4 bunch Italian parsley
2 bay leaves
12 whole black peppercorns
2 tbsp olive oil
1 red onion, chopped

2 stalks celery, diced
2 carrots, diced
1 large parsnip, peeled and diced
1/2 lb. rutabagas, peeled and diced
2 cloves garlic, minced
2 tbsp minced Italian parsley
salt and black pepper to taste
1 C. uncooked orzo pasta

Directions

1. In a large pan, add the turkey carcass and water on high heat and bring to a boil, discarding any foam from the top.
2. Add the chopped celery, chopped carrots, chopped Spanish onion, 1/4 bunch parsley, bay leaves and peppercorns and bring to a simmer.
3. Reduce the heat to medium-low and simmer, uncovered for about 3 hours.
4. Through a mesh sieve, strain the turkey broth and skim off any fat from the surface.
5. In a large pan, heat the olive oil on medium heat and sauté the red onion for about 5 minutes.
6. Add the diced celery, diced carrots, parsnip and rutabaga and cook for about 5 minutes.
7. Stir in the garlic and chopped parsley and cook for about 1 minute.
8. Add the turkey broth, salt and pepper and bring to a boil on high heat.
9. Reduce the heat to medium-low and simmer for about 15-20 minutes.
10. Stir in the orzo and cook for about 7 minutes. Cover the pan and immediately, remove from the heat. Keep aside, covered for about 5 minutes before serving.

HOW TO MAKE
Turkey Soup

 Prep Time: 30 mins
Total Time: 2 hrs

Servings per Recipe: 8
Calories	404 kcal
Fat	16.7 g
Carbohydrates	32.2g
Protein	29.9 g
Cholesterol	91 mg
Sodium	1067 mg

Ingredients

1 picked over turkey carcass
12 C. water
1 1/2 C. chopped celery
5 carrots
1 yellow onion, cut into wedges
2 tsp salt
3/4 tsp dried thyme
1 cube chicken bouillon
1 bay leaf
6 tbsp all-purpose flour
1/2 C. milk
1 small rutabaga, cubed

1/2 tsp ground black pepper
1 1/2 lb. cooked turkey, cubed
1/2 C. chopped fresh parsley
2 slices white bread, quartered
1 1/4 C. all-purpose flour
1 tsp baking powder
1/4 tsp salt
1/2 C. milk
4 tbsp butter, melted

Directions

1. In a large pan, add the turkey carcass, water, 1 C. of the celery, 2 carrots, onion, 2 tsp of the salt, thyme, bouillon and bay leaf and bring to a boil.
2. Reduce the heat and simmer for about 1 1/2 hours.
3. Strain the stock and discard the solids.
4. Keep aside to cool and skim off the fat from the surface.
5. Remove the meat from the bones and reserve it.
6. In a jar, add 6 tbsp of the flour and 1/2 C. of the milk.
7. Secure the jar with the lid and shake well to combine.
8. Add the stock in the pan and bring to a simmer.
9. Through a sieve, strain the flour mixture into pan, stirring continuously.
10. Slice the remaining 3 carrots.
11. Add rutabaga, ground pepper, remaining 1/2 C. celery, and sliced carrots in the pan and

simmer for about 20 minutes.

12. For the dumplings in a food processor, add the parsley and bread and pulse till medium sized crumbs form.

13. Add 1 1/4 C. of the flour, baking powder and salt and pulse till just well combined.

14. Add 1/2 C. of the milk and butter and pulses till just combined.

15. With mounded tbsp, drop the mixture into simmering soup.

16. Now, cook, covered for about 12 minutes.

17. Add the turkey meat and cook for about 3 minutes.

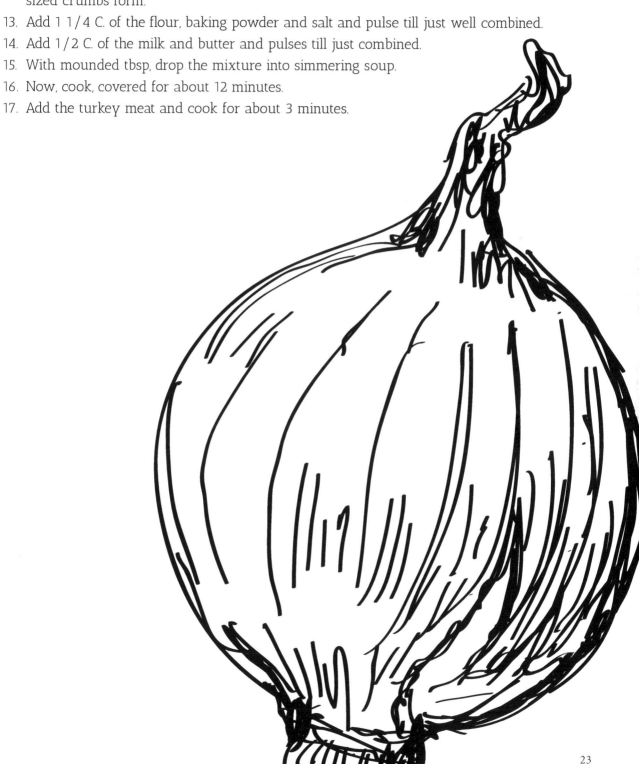

BUTTERNUT
Roast

Prep Time: 30 mins
Total Time: 1 hr 15 mins

Servings per Recipe: 10
Calories	210 kcal
Fat	6 g
Carbohydrates	38.9 g
Protein	3.5 g
Cholesterol	0 mg
Sodium	121 mg

Ingredients

1 butternut squash - peeled, seeded and cut into 1-inch dice
3 carrots, cut into 1 inch pieces
1 large sweet potato, cut into 1-inch cubes
1 rutabaga, peeled and cut into 1-inch pieces

3 parsnips, peeled and cubed
3 turnips, peeled and cut into 1-inch dice
1/4 C. extra virgin olive oil
kosher salt and pepper to taste

Directions

1. Set your oven to 450 degrees F before doing anything else.
2. In a large bowl, add all the ingredients and toss to coat well.
3. Transfer the vegetable mixture into a deep roasting pan.
4. Cook in the oven for about 45 minutes, stirring once in the middle way.

Rutabaga Bowl

🥣 Prep Time: 1 hr
🕐 Total Time: 6 hrs

Servings per Recipe: 12

Calories	417 kcal
Fat	13 g
Carbohydrates	65.8g
Protein	13.7 g
Cholesterol	29 mg
Sodium	896 mg

Ingredients

1 whole (10 lb.) Cinderella pumpkin
1 (16 oz.) package kielbasa sausage, sliced into 1/2 inch pieces, optional
3 carrots, peeled and sliced
2 celery ribs, chopped
1 large onion, peeled and chopped
3 cloves garlic - minced
2 C. parsnips, peeled and cubed (optional)
2 C. rutabagas, peeled and cubed (optional)
2 C. cabbage, coarsely chopped (optional)
1 green bell pepper, chopped
1 red bell pepper, chopped
1 head broccoli, cut into florets

2 zucchini, cut into chunks
1 1/2 C. canned or frozen corn
2 (13.75 oz.) cans chicken broth
2 C. cooked white or brown rice (optional)
1/2 C. chopped fresh parsley
1/2 tsp red pepper flakes,
1/2 (1.25 oz.) envelope dry onion soup mix
1/2 (1 oz.) packet dried Italian seasoning
salt and ground black pepper to taste

Directions

1. Set your oven to 400 degrees F before doing anything else and line a baking sheet with a piece of the foil.
2. Cut around the top of the pumpkin to make a lid.
3. With a large metal spoon, scoop out the inside membrane and seeds.
4. Arrange the pumpkin onto the prepared baking sheet.
5. Cook in the oven for about 1 hour.
6. Now, set your oven to 325 degrees F.
7. Meanwhile, heat a deep pan on medium-high heat and cook the sausage for about 10-12 minutes, flipping occasionally.
8. Stir in the carrots, celery, onion and garlic and cook for about 5 minutes.
9. Stir in the parsnips, rutabaga, and cabbage and cook for about 5 minutes.

10. Add the red and green peppers, broccoli, zucchini, corn, broth and rice and cook for about 5 minutes.

11. Stir in the parsley, red pepper flakes, onion soup mix, Italian seasoning, salt and pepper and remove from the heat.

12. Place the vegetables mixture into the pumpkin and cover with the pumpkin lid.

13. Loosely cover the pumpkin with a piece of foil.

14. Cook in the oven for about 4 hours.

15. Remove from the oven and scoop some of the pumpkin flesh from the sides and mix with the vegetable mixture.

Fall-Time
Roasted Vegetables

Prep Time: 10 mins
Total Time: 55 mins

Servings per Recipe: 14
Calories	135 kcal
Fat	2.6 g
Carbohydrates	27.4g
Protein	2.8 g
Cholesterol	0 mg
Sodium	116 mg

Ingredients

parsnips, peeled
6 large carrots, peeled
1 celery root, peeled
1 rutabaga, peeled
1 yellow onion, peeled
3 tbsp minced garlic

3 tbsp dried rosemary
2 tbsp extra-virgin olive oil
sea salt and freshly ground black pepper to taste

Directions

1. Set your oven to 400 degrees F before doing anything else.
2. Cut the parsnips, carrots, celery root, rutabaga and yellow onion into 1-inch pieces and place in a large sealable bag.
3. Add the garlic, rosemary, olive oil, salt and pepper and shake well to coat vegetables evenly.
4. In 2 (13x9-inch) baking dish, arrange the vegetables in a single layer.
5. Place the remaining oil and seasonings from bag over the vegetables.
6. Cook in the oven for about 45 minutes.

SWEET POTATO
Festival

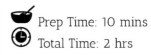

Prep Time: 10 mins
Total Time: 2 hrs

Servings per Recipe: 8
Calories	296 kcal
Fat	5.1 g
Carbohydrates	55.8g
Protein	4.2 g
Cholesterol	11 mg
Sodium	192 mg

Ingredients

3 tbsp butter
3 C. apple juice
1 C. dry white wine
1 1/4 lb. turnips
1 1/4 lb. parsnip
1 1/4 lb. carrots
1 1/4 lb. sweet potatoes

1 1/4 lb. rutabagas
salt and pepper to taste

Directions

1. In a large pan, add the apple juice and bring to a boil, then cook for about 30 minutes.
2. Add the butter and beat till well combined.
3. Set your oven to 425 degrees F.
4. Peel and cut the vegetables into 1/2-inch pieces.
5. Place the vegetable mixture in 2 roasting pans evenly.
6. Place the apple juice mixture over the vegetables and sprinkle with the salt and pepper, then toss to coat.
7. Cook in the oven for about 40 minutes.

Megan's
Chuck Steak Dinner

Prep Time: 1 hr
Total Time: 2 hrs

Servings per Recipe: 6
Calories	887 kcal
Fat	55.3 g
Carbohydrates	72g
Protein	25 g
Cholesterol	48 mg
Sodium	762 mg

Ingredients

3 1/2 C. all-purpose flour, sifted
1 1/2 tsp salt
1 C. shortening
1 C. cold water
1 lb. boneless round or chuck steak, cut into 1-inch cubes
2 potatoes, peeled and cubed

1 onion, chopped
1/4 rutabaga, cubed
1 carrots, diced (optional)
salt and pepper to taste
6 tbsp margarine

Directions

1. In a large bowl, mix together the flour and salt.
2. With a pastry cutter, cut in the shortening till a coarse crumbs like mixture forms.
3. Add the water and mix till a ball like dough forms.
4. With a plastic wrap, cover the dough and refrigerate.
5. Set your oven to 350 degrees F and line a baking sheet with a parchment paper.
6. In a large bowl, mix together the meat, potatoes, onion, rutabaga, chopped carrots, salt and pepper.
7. Divide the dough into 6 portions and shape each one into a ball.
8. Place the balls onto a lightly floured surface and roll into a 6-inch round.
9. Place about 1 C. of the filling over one half of each circle.
10. Dot each portion of filling with 1 tbsp of the margarine.
11. Turn other half of the pastry over the filling and crimp the edges to seal the filling.
12. With a fork, prick the pastries and arrange onto the prepared baking sheet.
13. Cook in the oven for about 1 hour.

WEDNESDAY'S
Dinner

Prep Time: 25 mins
Total Time: 1 hr 25 mins

Servings per Recipe: 8

Calories	164 kcal
Fat	2 g
Carbohydrates	30.4g
Protein	7.7 g
Cholesterol	0 mg
Sodium	321 mg

Ingredients

2 tsp canola oil
1/2 onion, chopped
3 C. water
1 green bell pepper, chopped
1 C. shredded carrot
1 C. cubed potato
1 C. corn kernels

1/2 C. chopped celery
1/2 C. chopped rutabaga
1/2 C. uncooked barley
3/4 C. dry lentils
2 C. chopped arugula
1 tsp salt

Directions

1. In a heavy Dutch oven, heat the canola oil on medium-high heat and sauté the onion for about 5 minutes.
2. Add the water, green bell pepper, carrot, potato, corn, celery, rutabaga and barley and bring to a boil.
3. Reduce the heat to medium-low and simmer, covered for 20 about minutes.
4. Stir in the lentils and simmer for about 30 minutes more.
5. Remove from the heat and immediately, stir in the arugula and salt before serving.

Rice Pudding
with Rutabaga

Prep Time: 20 mins
Total Time: 1 hr 50 mins

Servings per Recipe: 8
Calories	126 kcal
Fat	3.2 g
Carbohydrates	21g
Protein	3.6 g
Cholesterol	52 mg
Sodium	338 mg

Ingredients

1 C. water
1/2 C. long-grain white rice
1 lb. rutabaga, peeled and cut into 1 1/2 inch cubes
1/2 C. milk
1 tbsp butter
1/4 C. white sugar

1 tsp salt
1/8 tsp ground black pepper
1 dash ground nutmeg
2 eggs, separated

Directions

1. In a pan, add the water and rice and bring to a boil on medium-high heat, stirring once.
2. Reduce the heat to low and simmer, covered for about 20 minutes.
3. Meanwhile in a large pan, add the rutabaga and enough water to cover and bring to a boil on medium-high heat.
4. Cook for about 10 minutes.
5. Set your oven to 350 degrees F and lightly grease a 2 quart casserole dish.
6. Drain the rutabaga and place into a bowl with the milk, butter, sugar, salt, pepper and ground nutmeg and mash till smooth.
7. Stir in the cooked rice and egg yolks, then beat till well combined.
8. In another bowl, add the egg whites and beat till stiff peaks form.
9. Fold gently into the rutabaga mixture.
10. Transfer the mixture into prepared casserole dish.
11. Cook in the oven for about 1 hour.

NORTH DAKOTA
Vegetable Roast

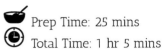

Prep Time: 25 mins
Total Time: 1 hr 5 mins

Servings per Recipe: 8
Calories	221 kcal
Fat	5.5 g
Carbohydrates	40.6 g
Protein	5.9 g
Cholesterol	0 mg
Sodium	565 mg

Ingredients

1 lb. new potatoes, halved
1/2 large rutabaga, peeled and cubed
1 large sweet potato, peeled and cubed
2 large parsnips, peeled and cubed
2 large carrots, peeled and cubed
3 tbsp olive oil
3 tbsp sweet red chili sauce

1 1/2 tsp onion powder
1 1/2 tsp garlic powder
1 tbsp steak seasoning
1 tsp ground black pepper

Directions

1. Set your oven to 375 degrees F before doing anything else.
2. In a large bowl, add the potatoes, rutabaga, sweet potato, parsnips, carrots, olive oil, chili sauce, onion powder, garlic powder, grill seasoning and pepper and toss to coat well.
3. Transfer the vegetables into a 13x9inch roasting pan.
4. Cook in the oven for about 40 minutes, stirring once in the middle way.

Root Vegetable Gratin

🥣 Prep Time: 15 mins
🕐 Total Time: 1 hr 55 mins

Servings per Recipe: 6
Calories   309 kcal
Fat   21.7 g
Carbohydrates   25.2g
Protein   5.8 g
Cholesterol   68 mg
Sodium   448 mg

Ingredients

2 Yukon Gold potatoes, scrubbed and sliced 1/8-inch thick with peel
1 turnip, peeled and sliced 1/8-inch thick
1 rutabaga, peeled and sliced 1/8-inch thick
1 small celery root, peeled and sliced 1/8-inch thick
1 parsnip, peeled and sliced 1/8-inch thick
salt
3 cloves garlic, minced

2 tbsp butter
1 1/4 C. chicken broth
1 C. heavy cream
1 tbsp chopped fresh thyme
1 pinch ground nutmeg
1 pinch cayenne pepper
2 tsp olive oil
1/4 C. finely grated Parmigiano-Reggiano cheese, divided

Directions

1. Set your oven to 375 degrees F before doing anything else and grease a 13x9-inch baking dish with 2 tsp of the oil.
2. In a large pan of lightly salted boiling water, cook the vegetables for about 3 minutes.
3. Through a colander, drain the vegetables and then immediately immerse in ice water for several minutes.
4. After cooling, drain well and keep aside.
5. In a large skillet, melt the butter on medium heat and sauté the garlic for about 3 minutes.
6. Stir in chicken broth, heavy cream, thyme, nutmeg and cayenne pepper and simmer for about 5 minutes.
7. Place the vegetables into the prepared baking dish evenly.
8. Place the broth and cream mixture over the vegetables and top with half of the cheese evenly.
9. With a piece of foil, cover the baking dish loosely and arrange onto a large baking sheet.

10. Cook in the oven for about 40 minutes.
11. Remove the baking dish from the oven and sprinkle with the remaining cheese.
12. Cook, uncovered in the oven for about 30 minutes.
13. Remove from the oven and keep aside for about 20 minutes before serving.

Handmade
Broth

🥣 Prep Time: 20 mins
🕐 Total Time: 1 day 3 hrs

Servings per Recipe: 12
Calories	154 kcal
Fat	3.1 g
Carbohydrates	23.8g
Protein	9 g
Cholesterol	12 mg
Sodium	248 mg

Ingredients

2 quarts water
12 oz. beef shank
2 large onions, chopped
2 large carrots, sliced
1 rutabaga, diced
salt and pepper to taste
4 potatoes, peeled and quartered

2 leeks, sliced
1 small head cabbage, sliced
2 tbsp chopped fresh parsley

Directions

1. In a large pan of boiling water, simmer the beef shank for about 1 1/2 hours.
2. Remove from the heat and keep aside to cool for overnight.
3. Lift the meat out and trim off the gristle, then cut meat into medium sized pieces.
4. Through a fine sieve, strain the stock.
5. Return stock to pan and bring to a boil.
6. Add onions, carrots, rutabaga, salt and pepper and simmer for about 1 hour.
7. Add the potatoes and simmer for about 15-20 minutes.
8. Stir in the leeks, cabbage, parsley and reserved meat and simmer for about 10 minutes.

GROUND BEEF
Rutabaga Dinner

Prep Time: 15 mins

Total Time: 1 hr 50 mins

Servings per Recipe: 8

Calories	231 kcal
Fat	9.2 g
Carbohydrates	23.9g
Protein	13.5 g
Cholesterol	43 mg
Sodium	370 mg

Ingredients

1 lb. lean ground beef
4 potatoes, diced
4 carrots, diced
1 onion, chopped
1/2 small rutabaga, diced
1/4 C. water
1 tsp salt

1/2 tsp freshly ground black pepper
4 tsp butter (optional)

Directions

1. Set your oven to 350 degrees F before doing anything else.
2. Heat a large skillet on medium-high heat and cook the beef for about 5-7 minutes.
3. Drain the excess grease from the skillet.
4. In a casserole dish, mix together the ground beef, potatoes, carrots, onion, rutabaga, water, salt and pepper and top with the butter.
5. With a piece of foil, cover the casserole dish.
6. Cook in the oven for about 30 minutes.
7. Stir well and add more water if required.
8. Cook in the oven for about 1 more hour.

How to Roast Rutabaga

Prep Time: 20 mins
Total Time: 1 hr 15 mins

Servings per Recipe: 12

Calories	426 kcal
Fat	14.6 g
Carbohydrates	68.5g
Protein	8.2 g
Cholesterol	0 mg
Sodium	415 mg

Ingredients

extra-virgin olive oil, plus more for greasing
4 russet potatoes, peeled and chopped into 1-inch cubes
1 rutabaga, peeled and chopped into 1-inch cubes
1/2 lb. baby carrots
1/2 large red onion, chopped into 1-inch pieces
1/2 large white onion, chopped into 1-inch pieces
1/2 lemon, juiced
3 cloves garlic, minced
2 tsp Italian seasoning
1 tsp lemon pepper
1/2 tsp sea salt

Directions

1. Set your oven to 450 degrees F before doing anything else and arrange a rack in the bottom of the oven.
2. Grease a large roasting pan with the olive oil.
3. In a large bowl, add the potatoes, rutabaga, carrots, red onion, white onion, 1/4 C. of the olive oil, lemon juice, garlic, Italian seasoning, lemon pepper and sea salt and toss to coat evenly.
4. Transfer the vegetable mixture into the prepared roasting pan evenly.
5. Cook in the oven for about 45 minutes.

GRANDMA'S
Pot Pie

Prep Time: 20 mins
Total Time: 1 hr

Servings per Recipe: 8

Calories	518 kcal
Fat	31.6 g
Carbohydrates	52.5g
Protein	7.4 g
Cholesterol	13 mg
Sodium	356 mg

Ingredients

1 3/4 C. sweet potato, peeled and cut into 2-inch chunks
1 3/4 C. red potatoes, peeled and cut into 2-inch chunks
1 3/4 C. rutabaga, peeled and cut into 2-inch chunks
1 3/4 C. carrots, peeled and cut into 2-inch chunks
2 tbsp olive oil
sea salt and ground black pepper to taste

1 tbsp butter
1 C. chopped onion
2 tbsp butter
1 1/2 C. vegetable broth
1/2 C. whole milk
3 tbsp all-purpose flour
1 1/2 tsp curry powder
1 (17.25 oz.) package frozen puff pastry, thawed and cut into four 5-inch squares

Directions

1. Set your oven to 400 degrees F before doing anything else.
2. In a roasting pan, add the sweet potato, red potatoes, rutabaga, carrots, olive oil, sea salt and black pepper and toss to coat well. Cook in the oven for about 20-30 minutes.
3. In a pan, melt 1 tbsp of the butter on medium heat and sauté the onion for about 3-5 minutes.
4. Add the sweet potato mixture, 2 tbsp of the butter, salt and black pepper and sauté for about 2 to 3 minutes.
5. In another pan, add the vegetable broth and milk on medium heat and bring to a boil.
6. Stir in the flour and curry powder.
7. Slowly, add the broth mixture into sweet potato mixture and cook for about 3 minutes, stirring continuously.
8. Transfer the mixture in 4 pot pie dishes evenly and top each one with a puff pastry square. Cook in the oven for about 17-20 minutes.

New-Age
Rutabagas

Prep Time: 20 mins
Total Time: 1 hr 20 mins

Servings per Recipe: 6
Calories   67.9
Fat   7.6g
Cholesterol   20.3mg
Sodium   67.1mg
Carbohydrates   0.0g
Protein   0.0g

Ingredients

1 large rutabaga
4 quarts water
4 tbsp butter

1/8 tsp black pepper
1/8 tsp salt

Directions

1. With a sharp paring knife, remove the wax coated skin from the rutabaga and cut into small cubes.
2. In a large pan of boiling water, cook the rutabaga for about 60 minutes.
3. Remove from the heat and drain well.
4. Transfer the rutabaga in a flat bottomed dish and with a potato masher, mash till desired consistency.
5. Add the butter, salt and pepper and mix well.
6. Serve immediately.

LENA'S
Favorite

Prep Time: 20 mins
Total Time: 40 mins

Servings per Recipe: 6
Calories	140.4
Fat	4.1g
Cholesterol	10.1mg
Sodium	58.7mg
Carbohydrates	26.7g
Protein	1.3g

Ingredients

4 C. peeled diced rutabagas
1/2 C. apple cider
3/4 C. halved cranberries
2 apples, cored and diced

1/4 C. dark brown sugar
1/2 tsp cinnamon
2 tbsp butter

Directions

1. In a large pan of water, cook the rutabaga till just tender.
2. Drain well and return in the pan.
3. Add the remaining all ingredients and simmer till well combined, stirring occasionally.

Dublin
Rutabaga

🥣 Prep Time: 15 mins
🕐 Total Time: 1 hr

Servings per Recipe: 6
Calories	192.3
Fat	12.5g
Cholesterol	20.3mg
Sodium	100.9mg
Carbohydrates	19.3g
Protein	2.7g

Ingredients

2 lb. rutabagas, peeled and cut into 3/4 inch cubes
salt
fresh ground pepper
4 -8 tbsp butter
CARMELIZED ONIONS
1 lb. onion, chopped
2 -3 tbsp olive oil

GARNISH
finely chopped parsley

Directions

1. In a heavy skillet, heat the olive oil on low heat and cook the onions for about 45 minutes.
2. Meanwhile in a pan of salted boiling water, cook the rutabagas till tender.
3. Drain well and mash completely.
4. Add the butter and beat well.
5. Stir in the caramelized onions and required amount of the seasoning.
6. Serve hot with a garnishing of the parsley.

RUDY'S
Butter Brown Veggies

Prep Time: 10 mins
Total Time: 30 mins

Servings per Recipe: 6
Calories   119.2
Fat   9.6g
Cholesterol   25.4mg
Sodium   146.4mg
Carbohydrates   8.1g
Protein   0.9g

Ingredients

3 large rutabagas, peeled and grated   1 tbsp brown sugar
5 tbsp butter
salt and pepper

Directions

1. In a large skillet, melt the butter and sauté the grated rutabagas till tender.
2. Add the salt, pepper and brown sugar. And stir till well combined.
3. Serve hot.

Pre-Colonial
Puree

🥣 Prep Time: 30 mins
🕐 Total Time: 1 hr

Servings per Recipe: 6
Calories   142.6
Fat   6.2g
Cholesterol   15.2mg
Sodium   160.6mg
Carbohydrates   21.1g
Protein   2.4g

Ingredients

2 lb. carrots, peeled and cut into 1 inch pieces
1 lb. rutabaga, peeled and cut into 1 inch pieces

3 tbsp softened butter
1 pinch sugar
salt and pepper

Directions

1. In a large pan of salted boiling water, cook the carrots and rutabagas for about 30 minutes.
2. Drain and with a potato masher, mash completely.
3. Add the butter, a pinch of sugar, salt and pepper and mix well.
4. Serve warm.

MASHED POTATO
Alternative

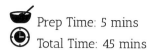

Prep Time: 5 mins
Total Time: 45 mins

Servings per Recipe: 2
Calories	130.1
Fat	6.7g
Cholesterol	17.4mg
Sodium	86.9mg
Carbohydrates	16.4g
Protein	2.8g

Ingredients

1 whole rutabaga
1 oz. milk
1 tbsp butter

salt
pepper

Directions

1. Peel and cube the rutabaga.
2. In a pan of boiling water, cook the rutabaga for about 40 minutes.
3. Drain and return to the dry pan on low heat to allow the excess water to evaporate off.
4. Add a little milk, a lot of butter, some salt and plenty of freshly ground black pepper and mash well.

5-Ingredient
Roots

Prep Time: 7 mins
Total Time: 27 mins

Servings per Recipe: 4
Calories	63.9
Fat	3.0g
Cholesterol	7.6mg
Sodium	44.7mg
Carbohydrates	8.7g
Protein	1.2g

Ingredients

1 medium rutabaga, peeled, diced 1/2 inch dice
1/4 tsp ground ginger
2 tbsp fresh orange juice
1 tbsp butter
salt & pepper

Directions

1. In a pan of boiling water, add the rutabaga and cook, covered for about 20 minutes.
2. Drain and Mash completely.
3. Stir in the remaining ingredients and serve hot.

SWEET RUTABAGAS
Euroland

Prep Time: 10 mins
Total Time: 40 mins

Servings per Recipe: 1
Calories	238.3
Fat	23.0g
Cholesterol	61.0mg
Sodium	167.1mg
Carbohydrates	8.9g
Protein	0.2g

Ingredients

1 small rutabaga
2 tbsp butter
2 tsp brown sugar

salt and pepper

Directions

1. Peel the rutabaga and cut it into 1/2-inch sized cubes.
2. In a heavy skillet, melt the butter on medium heat and sauté the rutabaga cubes till browned from all sides, stirring occasionally.
3. Add the sugar and reduce the heat to low.
4. Cook, covered for about 20-30 minutes, stirring occasionally.
5. Stir in the salt and pepper and serve.

Country Wagon Stew

Prep Time: 5 mins
Total Time: 48 mins

Servings per Recipe: 4
Calories	281.8
Fat	11.2g
Cholesterol	109.7mg
Sodium	693.0mg
Carbohydrates	17.1g
Protein	27.0g

Ingredients

1 small rutabaga, peeled and diced in 1/2-inch pieces
2 medium parsnips, peeled and diced in 1/2-inch pieces
1 medium carrot, peeled and diced in 1/2-inch pieces
2 tbsp butter
1 lb. boneless skinless chicken thighs, cut into bite-size pieces

1/3 C. flour
1/4 tsp salt
1/4 tsp pepper
1 large leek, chopped
2 C. chicken broth
2 tbsp chopped fresh Italian parsley, chopped

Directions

1. In a large pan of lightly salted boiling water, add the rutabaga, parsnips and carrot and cook, covered for about 10 minutes.
2. Drain well and keep aside.
3. Sprinkle the chicken with flour, salt and pepper, reserving any leftover flour.
4. Meanwhile in a large pan, melt the butter on medium heat and sear the chicken in 2 batches till browned.
5. Transfer the chicken into a bowl.
6. In the same pan, add the leek and sauté for about 3 minutes.
7. Add 1 tbsp of the reserved flour and stir till a paste forms.
8. Stir in the chicken broth and bring to a boil, stirring occasionally.
9. Add the chicken, vegetables and reduce the heat to low.
10. Simmer, covered for about 10 minutes.
11. Serve with a sprinkling of the chopped parsley.

EASY
Irish Dinner

Prep Time: 30 mins
Total Time: 3 hrs 30 mins

Servings per Recipe: 6
Calories	918.2
Fat	44.2g
Cholesterol	222.1mg
Sodium	3837.8mg
Carbohydrates	83.0g
Protein	48.6g

Ingredients

1 (3 lb.) corned beef brisket
1 head cabbage
2 large onions
1 1/2 lb. small red potatoes
4 carrots
2 parsnips
1 (2 lb.) rutabagas

3 C. unsweetened apple juice
1/2 C. light brown sugar
1 tbsp mustard seeds
1 tbsp kosher salt
1 tsp fresh ground black pepper

Directions

1. In a large pan, add the beef, 3 C. of the apple juice and enough cold water to cover the beef and bring to a boil on high heat.
2. Add 1/2 C. of the brown sugar and mustard seeds and again bring to a boil, skimming off any fat from the top surface.
3. Reduce the heat and simmer, covered for about 2 hours.
4. Cut some wedges off the cabbage.
5. Peel the carrots and cut into chunks.
6. Peel the parsnips and cut into chunks.
7. Peel a couple of onions but leave the root end on.
8. Cut the onions in half through the root end, then in half again, through the root end.
9. Peel the rutabaga and cut into chunks.
10. In the pan of beef, add all the vegetables except the cabbage and increase the heat to high.
11. Bring to a boil and stir in the kosher salt and black pepper.
12. Add half of the apple juice and half of the water and bring to a boil.
13. Reduce the heat and simmer, covered for about 15 minutes.
14. Uncover and stir in the cabbage.

15. Increase the heat to high and bring to a boil.
16. Reduce the heat and simmer for about 20-25 minutes.
17. Transfer the corned beef onto a chopping board and carve it.
18. Transfer the carved beef into a platter.
19. Transfer the vegetables into another platter and serve alongside the salt, pepper and butter.

LEEK, CELERY, and Tomato Soup

Prep Time: 20 mins
Total Time: 1 hr 10 mins

Servings per Recipe: 6
Calories	157.5
Fat	2.8g
Cholesterol	0.0mg
Sodium	367.0mg
Carbohydrates	31.9g
Protein	3.9g

Ingredients

1 tbsp olive oil
1 1/2 C. chopped leeks (white and pale green parts only)
1/2 C. chopped celery
1 garlic clove, minced
2 C. peeled turnips, 1/2-inch pieces
2 C. peeled rutabagas, 1/2-inch pieces
2 C. peeled russet potatoes, 1/2-inch pieces

2 C. carrots, sliced
1 (28 oz.) cans diced tomatoes with juice
4 (14 1/2 oz.) cans vegetable broth or 4 (14 1/2 oz.) cans low chicken broth

Directions

1. In a heavy large pan, heat the oil on medium-low heat and sauté the leek, celery and garlic for about 5 minutes.
2. Add the turnips, rutabagas, potatoes, carrots, tomatoes with juices and 2 cans of the broth and bring to a boil.
3. Reduce the heat and simmer, covered for about 45 minutes.
4. Transfer about 4 C. of the soup into a food processor and pulse till almost smooth.
5. Return the pureed soup to the pan.
6. Add the remaining 2 cans of the broth and bring to a simmer.
7. Season with the salt and pepper and serve.

February
Veggie Combo

Prep Time: 20 mins
Total Time: 45 mins

Servings per Recipe: 4
Calories   274.0
Fat   23.8g
Cholesterol   61.3mg
Sodium   781.7mg
Carbohydrates   14.2g
Protein   3.3g

Ingredients

1 C. chopped turnip
2 C. chopped rutabagas
1/2 C. chopped carrot
1 C. chopped broccoli
1 C. Brussels sprout
3 C. water

1/4 lb. butter
2 tbsp chicken-flavored broth
2 tbsp Mrs. Dash seasoning mix, blend

Directions

1. Peel and chop the turnips, rutabaga and carrots and cut into bite sized pieces.
2. Trim the Brussels sprout and remove the damaged leaves.
3. Chop the crowns of broccoli and then chop the stems.
4. In the bottom of a large colander, place the turnips and rutabaga, followed by the carrots, Brussels sprout and broccoli.
5. In a 3 quart pan, mix together about 4 C. of the water and 2 tbsp of the Soup Base.
6. Arrange the colander in the pan of water.
7. Sprinkle the vegetable mixture with Mrs. Dash seasoning and top with the butter.
8. Cover the pan, setting the lid slightly off-center to vent your steam and bring to a boil.
9. Reduce the heat to medium-high and steam for about 20-25 minutes.

POT ROAST
Skillet

Prep Time: 20 mins
Total Time: 3 hrs 20 mins

Servings per Recipe: 8
Calories	531.5
Fat	31.4g
Cholesterol	115.6mg
Sodium	228.8mg
Carbohydrates	26.2g
Protein	34.6g

Ingredients

3 lb. pot roast, as round as you can find
1 tbsp McCormick's Montreal Brand
steak seasoning
4 potatoes, scrubbed and peeled and
quartered
1 turnip, scrubbed and pared
1/2 onion, sliced in big chunks
2 C. carrots, pared (and chunked)
1 C. rutabaga, diced

1 celery rib, peeled (and chunked)
1 dozen button mushroom
SAUCE: TO 1 C. BOILING WATER ADD
2 tsp beef base
2 tsp mushrooms, base
1 C. tomato juice
1 sprig thyme
parsley (to garnish)

Directions

1. Set your oven to 375 degrees F before doing anything else.
2. Season the roast with steak seasoning evenly.
3. Heat a cast iron pan and sear the roast till browned completely.
4. Add the remaining ingredients and stir to combine.
5. In a bowl, mix together all the sauce ingredients.
6. Pour the sauce mixture over the roast mixture evenly.
7. Cover the pan tightly and cook in the oven for about 3 hours.
8. Transfer the meat and veggies into a warm platter.
9. Thicken the sauce according to your liking.
10. Serve the meat mixture with a sprinkling of the parsley alongside the sauce.

Parisian
Veggie Bake

🥣 Prep Time: 1 hr
🕐 Total Time: 2 hrs 15 mins

Servings per Recipe: 4
Calories	220.6
Fat	1.2g
Cholesterol	0.0mg
Sodium	1234.5mg
Carbohydrates	49.0g
Protein	9.4g

Ingredients

3 large white potatoes
1/2 medium brown onion
2 - 3 large carrots, peeled
1 large rutabaga, peeled
2 large zucchini
12 oz. sliced mushrooms
1 green bell pepper, seeded and stemmed
3 garlic cloves
2 beefsteak tomatoes
1 lb. thin cut beef (optional)

1 (8 oz.) cans tomato sauce
1 tsp beef bouillon powder
8 oz. water
2 tbsp pepper
1 tsp salt
1 tsp onion powder
1 tsp crushed basil
1 bay leaf

Directions

1. Set your oven to 350 degrees F before doing anything else.
2. Cut the potatoes, zucchini and bell pepper into 1/4-inch thick slices.
3. Cut the carrots, tomato and rutabaga into 1/8-inch thick slices.
4. Cut the onion thin slices.
5. Cut the beef into 1-1 1/2-inch wide, 2-inch long and n 1/4-inch thick strips.
6. In a baking dish, arrange half of the potato, carrot, onion and bell pepper.
7. Then, arrange half of the rutabaga and sprinkle with about 1 tsp of the pepper.
8. Then, arrange half of the zucchini, mushrooms, beef and tomato and sprinkle with 1/2 tsp of the salt.
9. Repeat the layers.
10. In a medium pan, mix together the tomato sauce, water, bouillon, bay leaf, basil, onion powder, 1 tbsp of the pepper and garlic and bring to a gentle boil, stirring continuously.
11. Remove from the heat and discard the bay leaf.
12. Gently, transfer the sauce mixture over the vegetables evenly.

13. Cover the baking dish and cook in the oven for about 45 minutes.

14. Uncover the baking dish and with the back of a spoon, gently push down the mixture.

15. Cover the baking dish and cook in the oven for about 30 minutes.

Cold Winter
Chowder

🥣 Prep Time: 15 mins
🕐 Total Time: 1 hr 15 mins

Servings per Recipe: 8
Calories	423.8
Fat	24.9g
Cholesterol	57.8mg
Sodium	666.2mg
Carbohydrates	40.1g
Protein	14.3g

Ingredients

250 ml cooked crumbled turkey bacon
1 7/8 liters prepared low chicken broth
500 ml water
750 ml rutabagas
250 ml diced onions
500 ml asparagus, cut in 1 inch pieces
10 ml chili powder
10 ml Cajun seasoning
2 ml basil
2 ml marjoram

250 ml frozen corn
500 ml table cream
2 (420 g) packages dry unprepared roasted garlic mashed potatoes

Directions

1. Cut bacon into 1/2-inch pieces.
2. Heat a skillet on medium-high heat and cook the bacon till browned completely.
3. Transfer the bacon onto a paper towel lined plate to drain.
4. In a large pan, add the chicken stock, water, bacon, onion and rutabagas and bring to a boil on medium heat.
5. Cook for about 20 minutes, stirring occasionally.
6. Add the asparagus and seasonings and cook for about 20 minutes, stirring occasionally.
7. Add the corn, cream and potatoes and cook for about 10 minutes, stirring occasionally.
8. Remove from the heat and keep aside for about 5 minutes before serving.

CARROTS, HARISSA, Peppers, Chicken, and Sausage Couscous

Prep Time: 45 mins
Total Time: 1 hr 30 mins

Servings per Recipe: 6

Calories	934 kcal
Fat	39 g
Carbohydrates	80.5g
Protein	62.2 g
Cholesterol	169 mg
Sodium	601 mg

Ingredients

3 tbsp olive oil
2 lbs chicken thighs
12 oz. Italian sausage, optional
1 tbsp diced garlic
2 onions, minced
2 carrots, julienned
1/2 stalk celery, chunked
1 rutabaga, parsnip, or turnip, chunked
1/2 green bell pepper, julienned
1/2 red bell pepper, julienned
1 can diced tomatoes
1 can garbanzo beans
2 C. chicken stock
2 tsps thyme
1 tsp turmeric
1 tsp cayenne pepper
1/4 tsp harissa, see appendix
1 bay leaf
2 zucchini, cut in half
2 C. couscous
2 C. chicken stock
1/2 C. plain yogurt

Directions

1. Brown your chicken thighs all over in olive oil.
2. Add in your sausage and cook everything until fully done. Once it has cooled dice the sausage into pieces.
3. Now stir fry your garlic and onions until tender and see-through then combine in: stock, bay leaf, carrots, harissa, beans, celery, cayenne, tomatoes, turmeric, rutabaga, thyme, red and green peppers.
4. Cook for 2 more mins before adding your chicken and sausage.
5. Place a lid on the pan and cook for 35 mins until chicken is fully done.
6. Add your zucchini and cook for 7 more mins.
7. Meanwhile boil 2 C. of chicken stock then pour it over your couscous in a bowl along with 2 tbsps of olive oil.
8. Place a covering on the bowl and let it sit for at least 10 mins.
9. When plating the dish first layer couscous then some chicken mix and then some yogurt.
10. Enjoy.

Rutabaga
Stew

 Prep Time: 20 mins
🕐 Total Time: 4 hrs 25 mins

Servings per Recipe: 15
Calories	111 kcal
Fat	2.1 g
Carbohydrates	12.9g
Protein	10.7 g
Cholesterol	23 mg
Sodium	80 mg

Ingredients

1 tbsp vegetable oil
1 1/2 lbs chicken, diced
4 rutabagas, peeled and diced
4 medium beets, peeled and diced
4 carrots, diced

3 stalks celery, diced
1 red onion, diced
water, or to cover

Directions

1. Stir fry your chicken in veggie oil for 4 mins.
2. Now combine in: red onions, rutabagas, celery, beets, and carrots. Submerge the contents in some water and get the mix boiling.
3. Once the mix is boiling set the heat to low, and simmer the stew for 4 hrs.
4. Make sure you continue to add some water during the cooking time to keep the veggies simmering.
5. Enjoy.

HONEY
Rutabaga
Couscous

Prep Time: 15 mins
Total Time: 35 mins

Servings per Recipe: 6
Calories	330 kcal
Fat	12.3 g
Carbohydrates	44.2g
Protein	11.7 g
Cholesterol	0 mg
Sodium	89 mg

Ingredients

1 rutabaga, chunked
2 C. water
1 tbsp vegetable oil
1 1/2 C. couscous
1/2 C. nutritional yeast
1/4 C. vegetable oil
1/4 C. apple cider vinegar
1 1/2 tsps honey
1 tsp Italian seasoning

1 tsp dried oregano
1 tsp dried dill weed
1/2 tsp ground black pepper
1/4 tsp cayenne pepper
1 pinch salt to taste (optional)

Directions

1. Steam your rutabaga over 2 inches of boiling water for 12 mins with a steamer insert.
2. Boil 1 tbsp of veggie oil with 2 C. of water then add in the couscous and shut the heat after placing a lid on the pot.
3. Let this sit for 15 mins before stirring after it has cooled.
4. Get a bowl, combine: cayenne, veggie oil, black pepper, vinegar, dill, honey, oregano, and Italian seasonings.
5. Add the rutabaga, couscous, and some salt to the dressing mix.
6. Toss the contents to coat everything evenly. Enjoy.

Homemade
Harissa (Classical North African Style)

🥣 Prep Time: 20 mins
🕐 Total Time: 20 mins

Servings per Recipe: 40
Calories   28 kcal
Fat   2.8
Carbohydrates   0.9 g
Protein   0.2 g
Cholesterol   0 m
Sodium   176 mg

Ingredients

6 oz. bird's eye chilies, seeded and stems removed
12 cloves garlic, peeled
1 tbsp coriander, ground
1 tbsp ground cumin
1 tbsp salt

1 tbsp dried mint
1/2 C. chopped fresh cilantro
1/2 C. olive oil

Directions

1. Add the following to the bowl a food processor: chilies, cilantro, garlic, salt mint, coriander, and cumin.
2. Pulse the mix until it is smooth then add in some olive oil and pulse the mix a few more times.
3. Place the mix in jar and top everything with the rest of the oil.
4. Enjoy.

HOMEMADE
Harissa (Classical Tunisian Style)

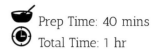 Prep Time: 40 mins
Total Time: 1 hr

Servings per Recipe: 192
Calories   10 kcal
Fat   0.3 g
Carbohydrates   1.9g
Protein   0.4 g
Cholesterol   0 m
Sodium   26 mg

Ingredients

11 oz. dried red chili peppers, stems removed, seeds, removed
3/4 C. chopped garlic
2 C. caraway seed

1/2 tsp ground coriander seed
2 tsps salt

Directions

1. Let your chilies sit submerged in water for 30 mins then remove the liquids.
2. Now add the following to the bowl of a food processor: salt, pepper, coriander, garlic, and caraway.
3. Puree the mix then place everything into a Mason jar and top the mix with a bit of oil.
4. Place the lid on the jar tightly and put everything in the fridge.
5. Enjoy.

Made in the USA
Columbia, SC
28 February 2025

54529800R00035